POOLS OF !
WAVES OF JOY

A MULTILINGUAL TAPESTRY OF HEARTFELT POEMS

AVNEET KAUR VIRDI

Copyright © Avneet Kaur Virdi
All Rights Reserved.

This book has been self-published with all reasonable efforts taken to make the material error-free by the author. No part of this book shall be used, reproduced in any manner whatsoever without written permission from the author, except in the case of brief quotations embodied in critical articles and reviews.

The Author of this book is solely responsible and liable for its content including but not limited to the views, representations, descriptions, statements, information, opinions and references ["Content"]. The Content of this book shall not constitute or be construed or deemed to reflect the opinion or expression of the Publisher or Editor. Neither the Publisher nor Editor endorse or approve the Content of this book or guarantee the reliability, accuracy or completeness of the Content published herein and do not make any representations or warranties of any kind, express or implied, including but not limited to the implied warranties of merchantability, fitness for a particular purpose. The Publisher and Editor shall not be liable whatsoever for any errors, omissions, whether such errors or omissions result from negligence, accident, or any other cause or claims for loss or damages of any kind, including without limitation, indirect or consequential loss or damage arising out of use, inability to use, or about the reliability, accuracy or sufficiency of the information contained in this book.

Made with ♥ on the Notion Press Platform
www.notionpress.com

For those who feel these words as deeply as their own memories, for those who find pieces of themselves in these verses, and for every soul to whom these lines are more than words—moments, echoes, and truths.

May this book be a reminder: you are not alone.

Contents

Preface ..... *vii*
1. Whispers Of Joy And Sorrow 1
2. Solitude's Gift: Friendship 2
3. Captaining Your Own Boat 3
4. Eternal Currents Of Life 4
5. Echoes Of Insight 5
6. Unstoppable Essence 6
7. The Shadows Within 7
8. Deserted Hopes 8

About the Author 9

Preface

During teenage years, life is a whirlwind of emotions, discoveries, and transformations. "Pools of Sorrow, Waves of Joy" is a reflection of my journey through this tumultuous yet beautiful period. Each poem in this collection is a piece of my soul, an echo of my experiences, and a whisper of my dreams.

Writing has always been my sanctuary, a place where I can explore the depths of my thoughts and the nuances of my feelings. This book is a result of countless hours spent in quiet contemplation, capturing moments of joy, sorrow, hope, and despair. Through these verses, I hope to connect with readers of all ages, offering a glimpse into the world as seen through the eyes of a teenager.

The themes of this collection are universal, yet deeply personal. They delve into the complexities of identity, the pain of growing up, the beauty of fleeting moments, and the constant search for meaning. Whether you are a fellow teenager navigating the same challenges or an adult reminiscing about your own youth, I hope these poems resonate with you and offer solace, understanding, and inspiration.

Thank you for joining me on this literary journey. I am grateful for the opportunity to share my voice and to invite you into my world. May these poems find a place in your heart and remind you that even amid chaos, there is always a whisper of joy and a promise of hope.

With heartfelt gratitude,
Avneet Kaur Virdi

1. Whispers of Joy and Sorrow

उसकी चुप्पी में ही उसका ग़म था,
उसके आँसुओं में ही उसका आनंद था।
न जाने क्या था, क्या राज़ छिपा था,
क्या यही हमारा इंतकाम था?

In her silence, sorrow's breath sighed,
In her tears, fleeting joy's light did bide.
What truth lay hidden, elusive yet clear?
Was this our path to solace's near?

2. Solitude's Gift: Friendship

जब उससे बात नहीं होती,
तब लगती है यह दुनिया छोटी।
अलग होकर तन्हाई ने पाया,
तो दोस्ती की राह से मुझे मिलाया।

When words falter and shrink the world,
In solitude's quiet, a friendship unfurled.

3. Captaining Your Own Boat

अपने सपनों को ऊँचाइयों तक लहराओ,
ख़्वाहिशों को हवा में उड़ान भराओ।
जब तक ख़ुद को न समझो, ना जानो,
अपनी पहचान को दूसरों की राहों में न उलझाओ।

People offer advice, let their wisdom flow free,
But remember, dear friend, to heed what you see.
For before you guide others, or bid them to roam,
First, forge your own path, and cherish your home.

4. Eternal Currents of Life

हम चलते जाते हैं,
बिना रुके बिना थमे,
पर वक़्त किसी के लिए रुकता नहीं,
पानी किसी के लिए थमता नहीं।
एक पल ठहरो,
जिंदगी ना निकल जाए कहीं।

We keep moving without pause or rest,
Yet time halts for none, it's a continuous quest.
Pause for a moment, lest life slips away,
Unnoticed and gone at the end of the day.

5. Echoes of Insight

अपने लवजो़ को एक बार दोबारा जाँच लो,
अपने आप को अंदर से पहचान लो।
जिसिसे करते हो प्यार, उनको परख लो,
अपनी जिंदगी को एक बार समझ लो।

Re-examine your words with care,
Recognize yourself, make sure you're aware.
Those you love, view with fresh sight,
Understand your life, see it in a new light.

6. Unstoppable Essence

तू नदियों सा बहता जा,
न थम किसी के लिए।
तू वक़्त सा चलता जा,
न रुक किसी के लिए।
अख़िर यह ज़िंदगी है,
तेरे ही जीने के लिए।

Flow like a river, never cease,
Move like time, never freeze.
For this life, finally see,
It's meant for you to simply be.

7. The Shadows Within

There is a part of me no one will ever know,
No matter how far back they go.
The truth is that it's too dark to see,
And it might scar them for eternity.
But that doesn't bother me,
As I am used to solitary.
I can deal with it on my own,
Because that is all I have ever known.
And some day far, far away,
I hope they can be happy seeing me that way.
That just might be a dream,
But one that has sure made me gleam.
However the dream is broken, welcome reality,
And I'd rather keep living in confidentiality.
Barring them it may seem,
It has just helped me not scream.
And one fine day, the truth will be revealed,
As that part of me is unconcealed.
Oh the joy it'll bring me,
as I'll finally be free.

8. Deserted Hopes

एक आरज़ू थी ख़ुदा से,
ख़ुशियों की बारिश, हो प्यार की बौछार।
पर जिंदगी जैसे सूखा रेगिस्तान,
गिरेगी न शांति कि वर्षा अबकी बार।
यह रूह उम्मीद जगाए बैठी है फिर भी,
की बूंदें छूएंगी इस धरती को जल्दी ही।

There was a wish for God above,
For rain of joy and showers of love.
But life feels like a desert dry,
Where peace won't fall from the sky.
Yet this soul yearns for that rain,
Hoping still, despite the pain.

About The Author

Avneet Kaur Virdi

At such a young age, Avneet Kaur Virdi is already making waves with a unique blend of youthful insight and profound wisdom. In "Pools of Sorrow, Waves of Joy" she captures the delicate dance of emotions that define the teenage experience. From the quiet whispers of solitude to the vibrant echoes of hope, this collection of poems offers a glimpse into the heart and mind of a young writer navigating the complexities of life. Through her literary work, Avneet aspires to provide solace, understanding, and inspiration, inviting readers to find a place in their hearts for her poems. Her gratitude for this opportunity to share her voice is evident, as she hopes her verses remind others that even amidst chaos, there is always a whisper of joy and a promise of hope. Join her on this literary journey and discover the world through her eyes—where every word is a step towards understanding and every verse a testament to resilience.

Milton Keynes UK
Ingram Content Group UK Ltd.
UKHW041900021224
451693UK00022B/70